D0897463

WELCOME

THIS JOURNAL IS THE KEY TO YOUR DREAM LIFE. IT WILL RAISE YOUR VIBRATION AND ALIGN YOU WITH EVERYTHING YOU DESIRE.

In order to see results, you MUST fill out one page EVERY night.

This journal belongs to:

———————◆————————

Table of Contents

Journal Overview

This journal is based off Law of Attraction principles. The Law of Attraction states that you attract into your life whatever you focus on. If you think and feel positively, you attract positive things. If you think and feel negatively, you attract negative things. Your thoughts and feelings become reality. You are what you feel and think about.

If you utilize the Law of Attraction correctly, you can manifest whatever you desire into your life. One of the most important steps in manifesting is to raise your vibration, which is the energy you are emitting into the Universe. This is key because high, positive energy attracts things that you want while low, negative energy attracts things that you don't want. The purpose of this journal is to help you raise your vibration by making you focus on the positives in your life and everything you are grateful for.

Once you raise your vibration, manifesting will come easier to you. In the first couple pages of this journal, I will go over the basic steps of the Law of Attraction, along with tips and tricks that will help you become a powerful manifestor. Then, I will go over the instructions for what you should write in this journal every night. Use the "Track Your Progress" page to track your progress from using this journal. As a complement to this journal, I have created both 1) a website (link below) that contains links to helpful Law of Attraction resources that align with sections of this journal and 2) playlists on my YouTube channel (link below) that also align with sections of this journal. My goal is to provide you with the necessary information about the Law of Attraction so that you can apply it correctly. I will constantly be updating both the website and playlists as I discover new, helpful resources.

I wish you nothing but the best as you start your journey towards a more positive life full of everything you desire. If you have any questions or concerns, email me at dreamlifejournal@gmail.com. Sending an infinite amount of positive vibes your way.

YouTube playlists :
www.youtube.com/channel/UC77nW6EUT4ebJ5UHStUWkcw/playlists

Website:
www.dreamlifejournal.wixsite.com/website

LAW OF ATTRACTION
Crash Course

If applied correctly, the Law of Attraction will materialize your dream life. In the following sections, I discuss how to apply the Law of Attraction effectively.

The Law of Attraction can be summed up into four words: Ask, Believe, Act, Receive. But like anything else, it's not that simple. The Law of Attraction is a way of life. It's a journey, a process- not a magic spell you can apply with the wave of a wand. It takes "work", but luckily, the work is uplifting and enjoyable. The following sections summarize the basic steps of the Law of Attraction.

LOA in 7 steps

1. SHADOW WORK AND LIMITING BELIEFS

Deep down, many of us have mental and emotional wounds/barriers/fears from past experiences- some of which we aren't aware of. These negative subconscious blocks present themselves as low vibrations within you, leading to negative thoughts, behavior and the attraction of negative energy into your life. This dark side of your subconscious mind and personality is called your "shadow". It's important to dig deep into your subconscious mind and bring awareness to your wounds and fears and work on healing or accepting them. Why? Because by bringing awareness to them, you bring your "shadow" to light, and so it ceases to be a shadow. You stop unconsciously attracting negative energy into your life. In the "Shadow Work and Limiting Beliefs" blog post of my website, I provide a few resources that further explain shadow work and how to perform it. Personally, I have found the following three things helpful in accepting and/or healing my shadow:

    i. <u>Therapy:</u> This one is obvious, but therapy definitely does wonders when it comes to not only bringing one's shadow to light but also in healing it. One online therapy option that I trust (from experience) is www.betterhelp.com.

    ii. <u>Journaling</u>: Complete journal prompts that will help you become aware of your shadow. On my website, I provided a link to a free shadow work journal that contains several prompts to write about.

iii. <u>Emotional Freedom Technique (EFT) Tapping</u>: EFT is an energy healing technique that has been shown to help treat depression, anxiety, symptoms of trauma, addiction, and other emotional and even physical problems. It's a simple technique in which you use your fingers to tap on specific energy points on your body while talking through the negative emotion or issue at hand. My favorite EFT YouTube channel is by Brad Yates. Simply type "EFT Brad Yates" into the YouTube search bar followed by whichever topic you would like to work on (anxiety, sadness, stress, anger, fear, worry, jealousy, forgiveness, self-love, health, money, or anything else you can think of), and you'll most likely find a video for that topic. Or, if you don't have anything specific in mind, go to "Brad Yates" YouTube channel, click on "Videos", then click on "Sort By," and click on "Most popular." Then, scroll through his EFT videos until you find a topic that you feel you should work on. I've also compiled some of my favorite EFT videos in the "EFT Tapping" playlist on my YouTube channel.

One specific aspect of your shadow that has been created by your past experiences and relationships are your limiting beliefs. The following is my favorite description of limiting beliefs from www.johnkennycoaching.com:

"Limiting beliefs are those things you believe about yourself that ultimately place limitations on your abilities. They are subconscious thoughts creeping in and telling you something that is ultimately not true. For example, "bad things always happen to me", "I'm no good at speaking to people", "all my relationships are painful", "I'd never make a good leader" or "I could never start my own business." Limiting beliefs are simply assumptions about your reality that come from your perceptions of life experiences. In order for our actions to have the greatest positive effect, we need to have beliefs that are as close to reality as possible. Deceiving ourselves with false realities and limiting beliefs could mean that we never fulfill our goals and dreams."

Some other common examples of limiting beliefs include "I'm not attractive enough", "I'm unlovable", "I'll only be successful if I overwork myself," "I'm not good with money", "I'll never be happy", and so on. If you truly believe these things about yourself, then you will attract them.

LOA in 7 steps

Hence, you MUST work on eliminating or changing these limiting beliefs in order to prevent from attracting experiences that validate these beliefs even further. The following are two ways in which you can change your limiting beliefs:

   i. One simple way to change your limiting beliefs is by affirming and visualizing the opposite belief. For example, while working on updating this journal, I realized I had the following limiting beliefs: 1) I'm not a morning person and 2) I have writing anxiety. Not only have I believed these two statements about myself for most of my life, but I also constantly say these statements out loud. After reading several articles on "limiting beliefs" (all of which are listed on my website), I began to realize that these two statements are just BELIEFS. They're true because I'm telling myself that they are true- not because of some gene I inherited that says I'm not a morning person or that writing papers makes me anxious. So, I decided that I would no longer say or think either of these phrases. Instead, I would affirm, "I love waking up early in the morning and getting work done" and "I love writing because it brings me peace and happiness." I now repeat these two phrases to myself a few times a day. Additionally, as I'm trying to falling asleep at night, I visualize myself waking up early in the morning, making a coffee, and FEELING excited to write out the sections of this journal. To my disbelief, after about a week of affirming and visualizing these things, I've been waking up easily everyday around 8 am and actually sitting down to write for hours. This is a drastic change for me, considering I would usually wake up around 2 pm and procrastinate until 12 am, only to write for 15 minutes. All this required took was recognizing my limiting beliefs and changing them by affirming and visualizing the opposite.

   ii. One other way to change your limiting beliefs is by listening to subliminals or affirmation videos at night while you're trying to fall asleep (or any other time), both of which you can find by searching on Youtube either "affirmations while you sleep" or "subliminals" plus the topic you want to work on. For instance, if your limiting belief is "I'm unlovable," then you'd search, "self-love affirmations while you sleep" or "self-love subliminals." Check out the Youtube playlist I've created called "Affirmations/Subliminals."

LOA in 7 steps

2. RAISE YOUR VIBRATION

To attract your desire, you must align your vibration/frequency with that of your desire. Unless you're trying to manifest something negative into your life, it is crucial that you raise your vibration to attract what you want. This is my favorite step of the Law of Attraction because not only does it help you attract your desires into your life, but it also improves the overall quality of your life. In order to "raise your vibration," you essentially have to do things that make you feel BETTER about yourself, your life, and your relationships. You have to do things that make you feel GOOD-engage in activities that are beneficial to your mental, emotional, and physical wellbeing. This is a step that must be worked on CONSTANTLY. The following are some of the ways in which you can raise your vibration:

i. **Practice positive thinking & gratefulness (the journal entries help with this)**
ii. **Meditate**
iiii. **Spend more time in nature**
iv. **Eat healthier foods (organic, unprocessed)**
v. **MOVE (walk, run, dance, do yoga, work out- get your blood pumping)**
vi. **Surround yourself with high vibe people (positive people that make you feel happy and loved)**
vii. **Avoid people who drain your energy (negative people who bring you down)**
viii. **Social media detox (avoid comparing yourself with others on social media)**
ix. **EFT Tapping videos on self-love, happiness, gratefulness, positivity, etc.**
x. **Compliment yourself and others**
xi. **De-clutter your living/work space**
xii. **Watch movies/shows/videos or read books that make you smile, laugh, and/or feel good.**
xiii. **Listen to music that makes you feel good**
xiv. **Repeat positive affirmations throughout your day**
xv. **SELF-CARE ACTIVITIES**
Technically all of the activities above could be considered as "self-care activities." In fact, the definition of self-care is "the practice of taking an active role in protecting one's own well-being and happiness," which is essentially what you should do in order to raise your vibration. On my website, I've included LONG lists of self-care activities. If possible, I suggest you practice AT LEAST one of these self-care activities everyday. To access this self-care list and more information on raising your vibration, check out the "Raise Your Vibration" blog post on my website.

3. DECIDE WHAT YOU WANT TO MANIFEST AND WHY

Take some time to figure out what you want to manifest and WHY. It's important to ask WHY you want to manifest a certain thing in order to figure out the underlying FEELING that you are desiring. This is the feeling that you must tap into in order to align your vibration with that of your desire. For instance, if you want to manifest weight gain or loss, is it because you want to feel more confident? If so, then this is the feeling that you have to tap into when you visualize or affirm your desire: confidence. You would have to practice building and radiating confidence throughout the day by affirming sentences such as "I am so confident in my healthy body" or by visualizing yourself feeling confident and proud of your body in a scenario where you typically wouldn't feel this way (i.e. at a pool party full of people you know). As another example, say you want to manifest your dream job. Why? How would this new job change how you feel? Maybe your current job is boring and unfulfilling. If this is the case, then the reason why you really want a new job is to feel excited and fulfilled. Tap into these feelings when you visualize working at your new job. In summary, decide what you want, ask yourself why (how will receiving this desire make you feel), and tap into that feeling when you affirm or visualize your desire (or preferably, tap into it as often as you comfortably can throughout your day).

4. ASK THE UNIVERSE

Once you decide what you want to manifest and why, ask the Universe for it. You can do this by asking for your desire out loud or writing a letter to the Universe. For instance, you could say/write, "Dear Universe, I ask that you bring into my life a funny, loyal best friend who loves to watch comedy movies just as much as I do. I would like this new friend so that I can have someone to tell my secrets to and someone to watch my favorite comedy movies with. We'll make each other feel heard and appreciated...." Go into as much detail as you like, especially on how this desire would make you FEEL if it were true. This only needs to be done ONCE. Afterwards, instead of asking the Universe for your desire, you THANK the Universe for it. Any new letters you write to the Universe should be along the lines of "Dear Universe, thank you for bringing my funny, loyal best friend into my life. She/he/they comes over every weekend and we watch my favorite comedy movies together..." You now thank the Universe for your desire as if it has already come true. You begin acting as if, which is step 5.

LOA in 7 steps

5. ACT/BE/FEEL AS IF

In order to attract your desire, you must act as if you already have it or are it. In other words, fake it till you make it. For instance, if you want to be financially wealthy, you must act as if you're rich, which can be as simple as feeling the emotions you would feel if you were rich throughout your day, saying or thinking affirmations such as, "I am a money magnet," and/or writing yourself a check in the amount of money you want to manifest and carrying this check with you at all times. This step aligns your vibration/frequency specifically with that of your desire. The following are a few ways in which you can "act as if". Do these things as often as feels natural to you (once a day/night, a couple times a week, etc.) You want to practice "acting as if" until it doesn't feel like you're acting. You'll feel in tune with your desire, you'll truly feel and trust that this desire is YOURS, that the Universe is bringing it to you. Once you reach this point of trust, you "let go" (see Step 7).

i. Affirmations

Affirm that you already have your desire (in your head, out loud, and, if possible, in front of a mirror). Each time you repeat an affirmation, try to FEEL the emotions you would feel if your words were true.

EXAMPLE 1: Camila wants to manifest her dream job at X company. She affirms "I love working at X," and "I am one of X's best employees." As she affirms this, she FEELS excited, proud, and confident.

EXAMPLE 2: Eric wants to manifest his dream body. He affirms "I love my healthy, strong body" and "I am so confident in my body." As he affirms, he FEELS strong, healthy, and confident.

EXAMPLE 3: Tatiana wants to manifest a loving relationship. She affirms "I am in a loving relationship" and "I give and receive love." As she affirms, she FEELS love, warmth, and comfort.

ii. Visualize

Visualize yourself receiving your desire. How would you react? How would you FEEL upon receiving it? Feel these emotions as best as you can while you visualize. Then visualize scenarios of you having your desire. What would you do with it? How would it change your life? How would it change your emotions? FEEL these new emotions! If visualizing is difficult for you, try writing this all down instead.

LOA in 7 steps

EXAMPLE 1: Camila wants to manifest her dream job at X company. She visualizes herself receiving a phone call from an X recruiter offering her the job. She FEELS the excitement and happiness that she would feel if the phone call were real. She then visualizes herself telling her friends and family the news. She visualizes herself working at X, sitting in her dream office, going in and out of work meetings, and talking to coworkers. She FEELS proud, successful, and confident.

EXAMPLE 2: Eric wants to manifest his dream body. He visualizes himself having his dream body in a scenario where he typically would be uncomfortable with his body (i.e. at the gym). He visualizes himself looking at his body in the mirror and admiring it and feeling proud of it. He FEELS the emotions he'd feel if he had his dream body: confidence, self-love, etc.

EXAMPLE 3: Tatiana wants to manifest a loving relationship. Tatiana visualizes going on dates with her partner and doing all the things she'd want to do with a partner. She FEELS the emotions she'd feel if she were in a relationship: love, joy, excitement, etc.

IMPORTANT NOTE: Remember, the goal in "acting as if" is to eventually feel as if you have already achieved your desire. In Eric's case (example 2), he must eventually and genuinely LOVE and appreciate his body, no matter how it looks or whether or not he's achieved his "dream body" yet! This is the KEY. He shouldn't "act as if" he loves his body for a couple minutes per day but then go back to hating it for the rest of the day. Why? Because the Universe picks up on Eric's hateful/negative energy about his body and returns it to him, meaning he'll stay stuck in this cycle of not loving his body. Additionally, if Eric loves his body, he'll be more inclined to nourish it by taking actions that benefit his health, such as eating healthier foods, going for daily walks, going to the gym, practicing proper hygiene, etc. But, don't let this worry you because, of course, Eric can't instantly and genuinely love his current body. It'll take time, and "acting as if" will help get him there. The point is: try to be aware of your thoughts and feelings throughout your day. In Eric's case, he should try to become aware of the negative thoughts about his body and counter them with positive ones.

iii. Prepare

Maya Angelou once said, "Ask for what you want, and be prepared to get it." You must prepare for the arrival of your desire. This could be as simple as making space for it in your home, buying something that you would need once your desire arrives, etc. This step is best explained through examples.

EXAMPLE 1: Camila wants to manifest her dream job at X company. She buys a picture frame to decorate her dream office desk with, and she goes through her closet to pick out the perfect business casual outfit for her first day of work.

EXAMPLE 2: Eric wants to manifest his dream body. He purchases a gym outfit that he wants to wear but currently doesn't because he doesn't have his "dream body" yet. For an even stronger effect, he wears this outfit to the gym.

EXAMPLE 3: Tatiana wants to manifest a loving relationship. She buys an anniversary card and writes a loving letter to her partner in it, describing all the qualities she loves about him/her/they (physical, personality, career, hobbies). She reads this card at night and feels the emotions that this partner would make her feel. She also engages in activities that she would do with a partner, such as going to the movies or to fancy dinner dates (with her friends or by herself). If Tatiana were looking for a more serious relationship, she could buy a toothbrush for her partner and place it in her bathroom and/or make space for her partner's clothes in her closet.

iv. Get others involved

Tell your close family members/friends to treat you as if you have already received your desire. If others "act as if" with you, it might make it easier for you to believe and trust that the desire is yours.

EXAMPLE 1: Camila wants to manifest her dream job at X company. She tells her mom to occasionally ask her, "How was work at X today?" When her mom asks her this, Camila responds by describing her ideal workday at X, "It was great. I presented my final report at today's meeting, and my boss loved it."

EXAMPLE 2: Eric wants to manifest his dream body. He asks his close family members to compliment him on his body with phrases such as, "You look great!" or "You look so strong and healthy."

EXAMPLE 3: Tatiana wants to manifest a loving relationship. She asks her close friend to ask her about her partner every few days with phrases such as, "What is your partner like?" Tatiana responds with a description of the qualities she wants in her partner.

v. Send yourself the news

Pretend to be the person who will grant you your desire. As that person, send yourself a text, email, or letter that congratulates you on having received your desire (or whatever you'd like the message to say).

EXAMPLE 1: Camila wants to manifest her dream job at X company. She sends herself an email with the subject line "X Job Offer" and the body text containing a fake offer letter from the company (generic offer letter that she found online and customized for herself).

EXAMPLE 2: Eric wants to manifest his dream body. He writes a note on his mirror that states "I love my body" and/or he sends himself a message from a fitness app he's been using that says, "Congratulations! You've reached your fitness goal."

EXAMPLE 3: Tatiana wants to manifest a loving relationship. Tatiana writes herself a letter from her partner's point of view, detailing how much he/she/they love Tatiana and saying anything else that Tatiana would love to hear from her future partner.

vi. Letter to the Universe

Write a letter thanking the Universe for your desire. Detail all the emotions your desire has made you feel and describe what you've done/are doing with your desire.

EXAMPLE 1: Camila wants to manifest her dream job at X company. Camila writes a letter to the Universe that states the following: "Dear Universe, thank you for guiding me to receive my dream job. Everyday, I get to work with coworkers and clients on X topic. I make X amount of money per year. My job makes me feel so excited to go to work everyday..."

EXAMPLE 2: Eric wants to manifest his dream body. He writes a letter to the Universe that states the following: "Dear Universe, thank you for helping me to achieve my dream body. Everyday, I feel so confident and strong in my body. I now feel confident when I workout at the gym...."

EXAMPLE 3: Tatiana wants to manifest a loving relationship. She writes a letter to the Universe that states the following: "Dear Universe, thank you for bringing me my perfect partner. Everyday, I spend quality time with him/her/they playing card games and going for walks. I love him/her/they so much, and he/she/they makes me feel so loved, appreciated, and supported...."

6. TAKE ACTION

This step is often overlooked by people trying to teach or practice the Law of Attraction, yet it is SO IMPORTANT! Here's the thing you have to keep in mind: you are CO-CREATING with the Universe. You must work WITH the Universe to transform your dreams into your reality. Action is the energy behind your intention! You must take the steps necessary that will bring you closer to your goal. For instance, if you're trying to manifest muscle mass gain, then you should start strength training and eating appropriately. Or, if you're trying to manifest a relationship, then you should sign up on dating applications or try to attend more social gatherings to meet new people. Or, if you're trying to manifest a new job, you should apply to different jobs, network with people that currently have your dream job, do things that will build your resume, etc. The specific action you should take depends on your goal. But generally, do what makes sense or feels intuitive to you. I have included helpful resources on how to take action in the "Take Action" blog post on my website, so make sure to check those out if you're having trouble with this step. I've also included a YouTube playlist on this topic. Feel free to email me at dreamlifejournal@gmail.com if you need help coming up with specific steps you should take to bring you closer to your goal.

7. TRUST AND LET GO

You have to believe in the Universe and trust that your desire is coming to you. Don't obsess, worry, or feel desperate about your desire because again, the energy you radiate is the energy you receive. If you emit desperate energy, you will either receive things that make you feel even more desperate or you will continue to lack your desire (and thus continue to feel desperate). A good analogy for trusting the Universe and letting go is the following: Order (or ask for) your desire like you would order food at a restaurant. When you order food at a restaurant, you don't stress about WHETHER your food is going to come or WHEN it's coming or HOW it's coming.

Instead, you KNOW for a fact that your food is on its way. You trust that your food is being made and that it will be delivered. You're prepared for your food. This is how you should feel about your desire. You should trust and KNOW that the Universe is bringing it to you. You might be wondering, "So at what point do I switch from doing things to manifest my desire (like affirming/visualizing) to letting go of my desire and trusting that the Universe will bring it?" This depends on you and how you feel. I suggest setting a time period (a few days or weeks) for when you will be performing the "act as if" activities. Then, once you feel that you are in tune with the vibration of your desire (when you TRULY believe that it is ours or that it's on its way), then you can relax or "let go." For instance, you could be affirming/visualizing a few times a day until you reach the point of complete trust in the Universe (that same feeling of KNOWING that your food is on its way at a restaurant). Once you reach this point, you can reduce the affirmations/visualizations down to once per day or once per week- whatever feels right. However, there are steps of the LOA that you should be performing constantly, including raising your vibration and taking action. You should always be doing things that make you feel good (such as practicing positive thinking and gratefulness by writing in this journal every night), and you should constantly be taking steps towards your goal (such as improving your skills, building your resume, or networking with the appropriate people for your dream job). Additionally, "letting go" doesn't mean forgetting about your desire- this un-aligns you with the vibration of your desire. Instead, the meaning of "letting go" is to not stress or worry about how/when/or whether your desire is coming. You must TRUST that it is yours! Do not overwhelm yourself when manifesting. Do what feels natural to you. If you feel you only need to visualize once per day, then do that. If you feel that writing in this journal every night is sufficient, then just do that. Personally, after years of manifesting my desires and seeing them come true, I have come to the point where I wholeheartedly trust that the Universe works in my best interest. So, the only "manifestation activity" I take part in everyday is writing in this journal every night, along with the occasional affirmations I think to myself throughout the day. Like with the other sections of this journal, I've included a blog post of helpful resources for "letting go" on my website. So, if you're feeling unsure on this step, make sure to check those resources out, or email me at dreamlifejournal@gmail.com if you have any questions.

inspirational
QUOTES

"See yourself living in abundance and you will attract it."

RHONDA BRYNE

"Whatever the mind can conceive and believe, it can achieve."

NAPOLEAN HILL

"ALL THAT WE ARE IS A RESULT OF WHAT WE HAVE THOUGHT."

Buddha

"When one door of happiness closes, another opens; but often we look so long at the closed door that we do not see the onen which has been opened for us."

Helen keller

"Be thankful for what you have, you'll end up having more. If you concentrate on what you don't have, you will never have enough."

OPRAH WINFREY

"See the things that you want as already yours. Know that they will come to you at need. Then let them come. Don't fret and worry about them. Don't think about your lack of them. Think of them as yours, as belonging to you, as already in your possession."

ROBERT COLLIER

"Nothing is, unless our thinking makes it so."

Shakespeare

" I attract to my life whatever I give my attention, energy and focus to, whether positive or negative."

CHARLES M. SCHULZ

"A person is what he or she thinks about all day long."

RALPH WALDO EMERSON

"When things soever ye desire, when ye pray, believe that ye receive them, and ye shall have them."

MARK 11:24

Affirmations
EXAMPLES

for WEALTH

1. Everyday I am becoming richer and richer.
2. Money comes to me easily and effortlessly
3. Wealth constantly flows into my life.

for LOVE

1. I am worthy of love and deserve to receive love in abundance.
2. I attract loving and caring people into my life.
3. I happily give and receive love each day.
4. I love myself.

for HEALTH

1. I am grateful for my healthy body.
2. I love and care for my healthy body.
3. Every day, my body becomes more energetic and healthy.

for CONFIDENCE

1. I am confident in my abilities and in the decisions I make.
2. I am doing the best I can with what I have, and it's enough.
3. My best keeps getting better as I learn and keep going.
4. I am strong, powerful and confident.

for SUCCESS

1. I am successful.
2. My goals and dreams always come true.
3. Today I will take steps towards realizing my dreams.

for HAPPINESS

1. I am happy.
2. I am allowing myself to feel happy all day, every day.
3. I will choose the happiness of this moment, instead of the pain of the past.

My FAVORITES

1. Everything works out for me easily and effortlessly.
2. Good things are always happening to me.
3. I am grateful for the many blessings in my life.

VISUALIZE

Every night, after you write in this journal... as you try to fall sleep, VISUALIZE your desire as if it has already happened. And most importantly, FEEL the emotions that you would feel if this desire were to come true. Emotions are energy in motion! Visualize and feel, and before you know it...your manifestations will be real.

MANIFESTATION TIP
CREATE A VISION BOARD

Download the Pinterest app, and create a vision board like the one pictured below. Include pictures of all your desires, and look through them everyday. This will help you visualize and keep track of your desires. Or, you can use the next page as your vision board. Glue pictures of your desires on there or draw your desires- whatever you prefer. Get creative with it.

MY VISION BOARD

Today's Positives

In this section, you will write positive things that happened to you TODAY- anything that made you feel good! The following is an example entry:

"I woke up in a good mood. I caught up with an old friend. I drank my favorite Starbucks drink. I got a good grade on my exam. I watched a funny movie that made me laugh a lot. Someone complimented my outfit today. The weather was nice. I had a productive day at work. I talked to my crush. I found a five dollar bill."

I am grateful for ...

In this section, you will write things that you are grateful for in life (not just today, but in general). These might repeat with every entry, but that's the point. Feeling grateful is vital in raising your vibrations. The following is an example entry:

"I am grateful for my family and friends, their good health and safety, my good health and safety, the roof over my head, the food on my table, my education, my job, my dog, Jhené Aiko's music, my comfy bed, my phone, etc."

Affirmations

In this section, you will write anything that you desire but as if it has already come true. The goal is that what you write in this section will one day be written in the "Today's Positives" section. The following is an example entry:

"I landed my dream job. I have the most loving, caring partner who also loves romance movies. I am beautiful, fit, confident, intelligent, and creative. I am rich. I have so many friends that share my sense of humor. I have a Tesla. I am traveling to Paris, France. I have all A's this semester. I am very positive and happy. I am great at making decisions."

Track Your Progress

EVERY NIGHT, FILL OUT A BOX WITH **G** FOR GOOD
DAY, **O** FOR OKAY DAY OR **B** FOR BAD DAY

week 1

week 2

week 3

week 4

week 5

week 6

week 7

week 8

week 9

week 10

week 11

week 12

week 13

week 14

week 15

week 16

The goal is to decrease your 'O' and 'B' days and increase your 'G' days.

Today's Positives

I am grateful for ...

Affirmations

Today's Positives

I am grateful for ...

Affirmations

Today's Positives

date: _____

I am grateful for ...

Affirmations

Today's Positives

I am grateful for ...

Affirmations

Today's Positives

I am grateful for ...

Affirmations

Today's Positives

I am grateful for ...

Affirmations

Today's Positives

I am grateful for ...

Affirmations

Today's Positives

I am grateful for ...

Affirmations

Today's Positives

I am grateful for ...

Affirmations

Today's Positives

I am grateful for ...

Affirmations

Today's Positives

I am grateful for ...

Affirmations

Today's Positives

I am grateful for ...

Affirmations

Today's Positives

I am grateful for ...

Affirmations

Today's Positives

I am grateful for ...

Affirmations

Today's Positives

I am grateful for ...

Affirmations

Today's Positives

I am grateful for ...

Affirmations

Today's Positives

I am grateful for ...

Affirmations

Today's Positives

I am grateful for ...

Affirmations

Today's Positives

I am grateful for ...

Affirmations

Today's Positives

I am grateful for ...

Affirmations

Today's Positives

I am grateful for ...

Affirmations

Today's Positives

I am grateful for ...

Affirmations

Today's Positives

I am grateful for ...

Affirmations

Today's Positives

I am grateful for ...

Affirmations

Today's Positives

I am grateful for ...

Affirmations

Today's Positives

I am grateful for ...

Affirmations

Today's Positives

date: _____

I am grateful for ...

Affirmations

Today's Positives

I am grateful for ...

Affirmations

Today's Positives

I am grateful for ...

Affirmations

Today's Positives

I am grateful for ...

Affirmations

Today's Positives

I am grateful for ...

Affirmations

Today's Positives

I am grateful for ...

Affirmations

Today's Positives

date: _____

I am grateful for ...

Affirmations

Today's Positives

I am grateful for ...

Affirmations

Today's Positives

I am grateful for ...

Affirmations

Today's Positives

date: _____

I am grateful for ...

Affirmations

Today's Positives

date: _____

I am grateful for ...

Affirmations

Today's Positives

I am grateful for ...

Affirmations

Today's Positives

I am grateful for ...

Affirmations

Today's Positives

date: _____

I am grateful for ...

Affirmations

Today's Positives

date: _____

I am grateful for ...

Affirmations

Today's Positives

I am grateful for ...

Affirmations

Today's Positives

I am grateful for ...

Affirmations

Today's Positives

I am grateful for ...

Affirmations

Today's Positives

I am grateful for ...

Affirmations

Today's Positives

I am grateful for ...

Affirmations

Today's Positives

date: _____

I am grateful for ...

Affirmations

Today's Positives

I am grateful for ...

Affirmations

Today's Positives

date: _____

I am grateful for ...

Affirmations

Today's Positives

I am grateful for ...

Affirmations

Today's Positives

date: _____

I am grateful for ...

Affirmations

Today's Positives

I am grateful for ...

Affirmations

Today's Positives

date: _____

I am grateful for ...

Affirmations

Today's Positives

I am grateful for ...

Affirmations

Today's Positives

I am grateful for ...

Affirmations

Today's Positives

I am grateful for ...

Affirmations

Today's Positives

date: _____

I am grateful for ...

Affirmations

Today's Positives

I am grateful for ...

Affirmations

Today's Positives

date: _____

I am grateful for ...

Affirmations

Today's Positives

I am grateful for ...

Affirmations

Today's Positives

I am grateful for ...

Affirmations

Today's Positives

date: _____

I am grateful for ...

Affirmations

Today's Positives

I am grateful for ...

Affirmations

Today's Positives

I am grateful for ...

Affirmations

Today's Positives

I am grateful for ...

Affirmations

Today's Positives

I am grateful for ...

Affirmations

Today's Positives

date: _____

I am grateful for ...

Affirmations

Today's Positives

I am grateful for ...

Affirmations

Today's Positives

I am grateful for ...

Affirmations

Today's Positives

I am grateful for ...

Affirmations

Today's Positives

I am grateful for ...

Affirmations

Today's Positives

date: _____

I am grateful for ...

Affirmations

Today's Positives

I am grateful for ...

Affirmations

Today's Positives

date: _____

I am grateful for ...

Affirmations

Today's Positives

I am grateful for ...

Affirmations

Today's Positives

I am grateful for ...

Affirmations

Today's Positives

date: _____

I am grateful for ...

Affirmations

Today's Positives

I am grateful for ...

Affirmations

Today's Positives

date: _____

I am grateful for ...

Affirmations

Today's Positives

I am grateful for ...

Affirmations

Today's Positives

I am grateful for ...

Affirmations

Today's Positives

I am grateful for ...

Affirmations

Today's Positives

I am grateful for ...

Affirmations

Today's Positives

I am grateful for ...

Affirmations

Today's Positives

date: _____

I am grateful for ...

Affirmations

Today's Positives

I am grateful for ...

Affirmations

Today's Positives

date: _____

I am grateful for ...

Affirmations

Today's Positives

I am grateful for ...

Affirmations

Today's Positives

I am grateful for ...

Affirmations

Today's Positives

I am grateful for ...

Affirmations

Today's Positives

I am grateful for ...

Affirmations

Today's Positives

I am grateful for ...

Affirmations

Today's Positives

I am grateful for ...

Affirmations

Today's Positives

I am grateful for ...

Affirmations

Today's Positives

I am grateful for ...

Affirmations

Today's Positives

I am grateful for ...

Affirmations

Today's Positives

date: _____

I am grateful for ...

Affirmations

Today's Positives

I am grateful for ...

Affirmations

Today's Positives

I am grateful for ...

Affirmations

Today's Positives

I am grateful for ...

Affirmations

Today's Positives

date: _____

I am grateful for ...

Affirmations

Today's Positives

date: _____

I am grateful for ...

Affirmations

Today's Positives

I am grateful for ...

Affirmations

Today's Positives

I am grateful for ...

Affirmations

Today's Positives

I am grateful for ...

Affirmations

Today's Positives

I am grateful for ...

Affirmations

Today's Positives

date: _____

I am grateful for ...

Affirmations

Today's Positives

I am grateful for ...

Affirmations

Today's Positives

date: _____

I am grateful for ...

Affirmations

Today's Positives

I am grateful for ...

Affirmations

Today's Positives

date: _____

I am grateful for ...

Affirmations

Today's Positives

I am grateful for ...

Affirmations

Today's Positives

I am grateful for ...

Affirmations

Made in the USA
Coppell, TX
03 May 2021

54873015R00077